The Power of Storytelling in Marketing

15 Strategies to Help You Craft Your Story

Copyright 2024 by-All rights reserved

No part of this publication may be copied, reproduced in any format, by any means, electronic or otherwise, without prior consent from the copyright owner and publisher of this book.

Table of Contents

Introduction 5

Chapter 1: Finding Your Brand's Voice 8

Chapter 2: Crafting a Compelling Brand Story 10

Chapter 3: The Hero's Journey in Marketing 12

Chapter 4: Emotion-Driven Marketing 15

Chapter 5: Storytelling Through Visuals 18

Chapter 6: Creating Content That Speaks 21

Chapter 7: The Power of Testimonials and Case Studies 24

Chapter 8: The Art of Persuasive Copywriting 27

Chapter 9: Building Community Through Stories 30

Chapter 10: Storytelling on Social Media 33

Chapter 11: Authenticity in Storytelling 36

Chapter 12: The Role of Customer Feedback in Your Story 39

Chapter 13: Storytelling in Email Marketing 43

Chapter 14: Storytelling for Small Budgets 47

Chapter 15: Measuring the Impact of Your Story 50

Conclusion: Your Storytelling Journey Begins 54

Introduction

In today's saturated market, where consumers are inundated with a relentless stream of advertisements and promotional messages, capturing and retaining their attention has become a formidable challenge for brands. Amidst this cacophony of marketing noise, only a select few brands manage to rise above the fray—those that succeed are the ones that tell compelling stories. These brands understand that in a world overflowing with choices, it's not enough to simply push a product; the real power lies in crafting narratives that resonate on a deeper, emotional level.

Storytelling in marketing transcends the traditional goal of merely selling a product. It's about creating a narrative that speaks to the heart of the consumer, one that they can see themselves in, and one that aligns with their values, aspirations, and experiences. A well-told story doesn't just inform or entertain—it forms a connection, a bond that goes beyond the transactional. It's this connection that makes a brand memorable, turning a fleeting interaction into a lasting relationship.

Consider the brands that have etched themselves into your memory. They likely didn't just tell you about the features of their products; they shared stories that made you feel something—hope, excitement, belonging, or even nostalgia. These stories weren't just about what the brand was selling; they were about how the brand fit into your life, your dreams, and your identity. This is the essence of effective storytelling in marketing: it's not just about what you sell, but about what you stand for and how you make your customers feel.

This book is designed to be your comprehensive guide to harnessing the immense power of storytelling to elevate your brand. Whether you're a seasoned marketer or someone just starting out, whether you have a large budget or are working with limited resources, this guide will provide you with the tools and strategies you need to craft narratives that engage your audience and drive meaningful action.

We'll explore the fundamental principles of storytelling and how they can be applied to marketing in practical, impactful ways. You'll learn how to develop stories that not only capture attention but also sustain it, creating a lasting impression that encourages loyalty and advocacy. We'll dive into the psychology of storytelling, understanding why certain narratives resonate more deeply than others and how you can use these insights to craft stories that are not only heard but remembered.

Throughout this journey, you'll discover how to tell your brand's story in a way that aligns with your audience's values, builds trust, and encourages emotional investment. We'll cover a range of techniques, from leveraging customer testimonials and user-generated content to creating immersive brand experiences that draw your audience into your narrative world. You'll learn how to adapt your storytelling to different platforms, ensuring that your message is compelling whether it's delivered through social media, email, video, or traditional media.

And perhaps most importantly, you'll learn that you don't need a massive budget or extensive marketing experience to tell a great story. Creativity, authenticity, and a deep understanding of your audience are far more valuable than a big marketing spend. This book will empower you to use storytelling as a powerful equalizer, allowing you to compete with larger brands by connecting with your audience on a human level—where the real magic happens.

By the end of this guide, you'll not only be able to tell your brand's story—you'll be able to tell it in a way that captivates your audience, builds lasting relationships, and drives the kind of meaningful action that leads to sustained success. Whether you're looking to boost sales, build brand awareness, or create a loyal customer base, the power of storytelling will be your most valuable tool.

Chapter 1: Finding Your Brand's Voice

Imagine walking into a bustling room full of people, each engaged in animated conversations. The room is alive with chatter, but it's difficult to focus on any one discussion because it all blends together into a noisy blur. Then, suddenly, a voice breaks through the din—a voice that is clear, compelling, and unmistakably speaking to you. It captures your attention instantly because it resonates with your thoughts, speaks your language, and aligns with your needs. This is the power of a strong brand voice. It's the distinct quality that makes your brand not only recognizable but also relatable, even in a crowded marketplace filled with competitors.

Your brand's voice is more than just a tone or style; it's the unique personality that your brand projects in every piece of communication. It's a deliberate blend of tone, language, and style, meticulously crafted to reflect your brand's core values and designed to connect deeply with your target audience. A strong brand voice doesn't just happen; it's cultivated by understanding exactly who you are as a brand, who your audience is, and how you want to engage with them on an emotional and intellectual level.

To start, you must first identify the core values that are at the heart of your brand. Ask yourself: What does your brand stand for? What principles guide your decisions and interactions? How do you want your audience to see and feel about you? These values are the foundation of your brand's identity and will inform every aspect of your communication strategy.

Once you have a firm grasp on these values, the next step is to articulate them in a brand voice document. This document serves as a roadmap, outlining the specific tone, language, and style that should be used consistently across all your marketing materials. Whether it's a tweet, a blog post, an advertisement, or customer service communication, your brand voice should be instantly recognizable and consistent.

As a challenge, commit to using this refined brand voice across all your marketing channels for the next month. Observe how it resonates with your audience, how it influences engagement, and how it distinguishes your brand in the marketplace. By consistently applying your brand's voice, you'll create a cohesive and compelling brand presence that not only stands out but also forges meaningful connections with your audience.

Chapter 2: Crafting a Compelling Brand Story

Think of the most memorable brands that have left a lasting impression on you. Whether it's Apple, with its story of relentless innovation and the pursuit of simplicity, or Nike, whose narrative of perseverance and human potential inspires millions, these brands have done something extraordinary—they've crafted stories that transcend the mere products they sell. They tell tales that tap into our deepest aspirations, our struggles, and our dreams, creating a bond that goes far beyond a transaction.

A brand story is much more than a chronological account of your company's history; it's a rich narrative that intricately weaves together your mission, vision, and values, along with the unique journey that has shaped your brand into what it is today. This story is the heartbeat of your brand, the essence that differentiates you in the marketplace and resonates with your audience on a profoundly emotional level. When done right, a compelling brand story doesn't just attract customers; it turns them into loyal advocates who are emotionally invested in your brand's success.

To begin crafting your brand's origin story, start by reflecting on the pivotal moments that define your journey. What were the key challenges you faced, and how did you overcome them? What inspired the inception of your brand, and what values have guided your decisions along the way? These moments are the building blocks of your narrative, providing depth and authenticity that will resonate with your audience.

Write a first draft of your brand's origin story with a focus on these defining moments. Don't just recount facts—bring your story to life with vivid descriptions, emotional insights, and a clear connection to your brand's mission and values. Then, share this draft with someone who closely represents your target audience. Their feedback will be invaluable in refining your story, helping you to identify what resonates most strongly and where you might need to clarify or expand.

Once you've gathered feedback, refine your story, ensuring it's both authentic and compelling. Test this refined narrative in your next marketing campaign and observe how it connects with your audience. By consistently telling your brand's story, you'll create a powerful, lasting connection with your customers—one that turns them from passive consumers into passionate advocates for your brand.

Chapter 3: The Hero's Journey in Marketing

Imagine yourself watching a captivating movie where the protagonist is thrust into a world of daunting challenges and overwhelming odds. You find yourself on the edge of your seat, rooting for them as they navigate each obstacle, grow stronger, and ultimately emerge victorious. There's something profoundly satisfying about witnessing their journey—from struggle to triumph—and it's this emotional arc that keeps you invested. Now, imagine if your customer could be the hero of such a story, with your brand playing the crucial role of the wise mentor or guide who helps them achieve their goals.

The Hero's Journey, a timeless storytelling framework used in literature and film, is the perfect blueprint for crafting compelling marketing narratives. This framework positions the customer as the hero, embarking on a quest to solve a problem or achieve a significant goal. Along the way, they encounter challenges that seem almost impossible to overcome. This is where your brand steps in—not as the hero, but as the trusted guide who provides the necessary tools, knowledge, and support to help them succeed.

To bring this narrative to life, start by identifying the most common challenges your customers face. What are the obstacles that stand in their way? What aspirations do they hold dear, and what fears or frustrations do they encounter on their journey? Understanding these pain points is essential, as it allows you to position your product or service as the solution—the critical aid that empowers your customers to overcome their difficulties and reach their desired outcome.

Next, craft a narrative where your customer is the hero of the story. Begin by painting a vivid picture of their situation before encountering your brand—the struggles, the doubts, the hurdles they face. Then, introduce your brand as the mentor figure, much like Yoda to Luke Skywalker or Dumbledore to Harry Potter. Your brand provides the guidance, tools, and wisdom that help the hero navigate their journey. Show how, with your brand's help, they are able to conquer their challenges, grow, and ultimately achieve their goals.

Incorporate this narrative into your marketing communications—whether it's through compelling ad campaigns, customer testimonials, or content that speaks directly to your audience's journey. By framing your customer as the hero and your brand as the guide, you create a story that resonates deeply with your audience. They see themselves in the narrative, understand how your brand fits into their lives, and are more likely to feel a strong, emotional connection to your message.

As you roll out this hero-centric narrative, pay close attention to how it resonates with your audience. Look for signs of increased engagement, stronger loyalty, and deeper emotional connections. When customers see themselves as the hero of their own story, with your brand by their side, you're not just selling a product—you're helping them achieve their own personal victories, which is the most powerful connection you can create.

Chapter 4: Emotion-Driven Marketing

Think about the last time you made a purchase that was driven purely by emotion. Maybe it was the joy of selecting the perfect gift for a loved one, the thrill of treating yourself to something special, or even the comfort of buying something that reminded you of a cherished memory. In that moment, it wasn't just the product itself that influenced your decision—it was the emotion it sparked within you. That feeling was the key driver, subtly guiding your choice and making the experience memorable.

Emotions are incredibly powerful in the decision-making process. They influence our choices in ways we often don't even realize. Whether it's the surge of joy, the comfort of nostalgia, the sense of security that comes from trust, or even the excitement of something new, emotions can transform a simple transaction into a meaningful experience. For brands, understanding and tapping into these emotions can make your marketing messages not only more persuasive but also more memorable.

To leverage the power of emotion in your marketing, start by choosing the specific emotion you want your brand to evoke. Consider the essence of your brand and the values you stand for— do you want to evoke a sense of trust and reliability, perhaps? Or maybe you want your audience to feel the thrill of excitement or the warmth of happiness when they interact with your brand. The emotion you choose will be the cornerstone of your campaign, guiding every element of your messaging, visuals, and overall approach.

Once you've identified the emotion, create a marketing campaign or piece of content that is specifically designed to evoke this feeling in your audience. For example, if you're aiming to evoke trust, your content might feature testimonials from satisfied customers, behind-the-scenes looks at your meticulous quality control processes, or stories that highlight your brand's long history and commitment to excellence. If excitement is your goal, you might focus on dynamic visuals, energetic language, and time-sensitive offers that create a sense of urgency and anticipation.

After launching your campaign, closely track the engagement and responses from your audience. Pay attention to key metrics like likes, shares, comments, and overall sentiment to gauge how effectively you've connected on an emotional level. Are people reacting the way you hoped? Are they sharing your content because it resonated with them emotionally? Use these insights to refine your approach, ensuring that your brand consistently evokes the desired emotion in your audience.

By deliberately crafting your marketing to tap into specific emotions, you're not just promoting a product or service—you're creating an experience that resonates deeply with your audience.

This emotional connection is what turns casual customers into loyal advocates, making your brand a meaningful part of their lives.

Chapter 5: Storytelling Through Visuals

Imagine scrolling through your social media feed, casually passing by a sea of posts, updates, and ads. What makes you pause, even for a moment? More often than not, it's a striking image, a captivating video, or a powerful visual that seizes your attention before you've even had a chance to read the text that accompanies it. In that split second, the visual either captures your interest or it doesn't—and if it does, it's done more than just catch your eye; it's communicated a message, stirred an emotion, or sparked curiosity.

This is the power of visual storytelling, a crucial element in modern marketing that goes beyond aesthetics. The right visuals can distill complex ideas into something instantly understandable, evoke a deep emotional response, and make your brand unforgettable in the minds of your audience. In an age where people are bombarded with information, the ability to tell your brand's story visually is not just an advantage—it's a necessity.

To harness this power, start by reviewing your brand's current visual assets. Take a close look at your logo, website design, social media content, and any other visual elements associated with your brand. Ask yourself: Do these visuals tell a cohesive and compelling story? Do they align with the core values and narrative of your brand? Are they consistent across all platforms, creating a unified experience for your audience? This audit is essential for understanding how your brand is currently perceived and identifying areas where your visual storytelling might be falling short.

Once you've assessed your visual assets, choose one element to update or create anew—something that can significantly enhance your brand's narrative. This could be a refreshed logo that better reflects your brand's evolution, a new website design that improves user experience while telling your story more effectively, or a series of social media visuals that consistently convey your brand's key messages. Whatever you choose, ensure it aligns with your brand's identity and helps to tell the story you want your audience to hear.

Next, integrate this updated or newly created visual into a marketing campaign. For example, if you've updated your logo, roll it out with a campaign that highlights your brand's journey and what the new logo represents. If it's a new social media visual strategy, use it to enhance a product launch or to tell customer stories that resonate with your audience. The goal is to see how this visual element enhances your brand's story and connects with your audience on a deeper level.

Finally, analyze the impact of this visual on engagement. Track metrics such as likes, shares, comments, and overall interaction rates. Did the new visual element increase your audience's engagement? Are people responding more positively to your content? Use this data to refine your visual storytelling strategy, ensuring that every image, video, and design element contributes to a cohesive, emotionally resonant brand narrative.

By thoughtfully crafting and updating your visual elements, you're not just making your brand look good—you're enhancing its ability to connect with your audience, tell its story, and leave a lasting impression in an increasingly visual world.

Chapter 6: Creating Content That Speaks

Imagine stumbling upon a blog post that feels as though it was written just for you. Every sentence seems to echo your thoughts, addressing your challenges and providing insights that feel almost tailor-made to your situation. As you read, you can't help but feel a sense of connection—you're understood, and because of this, you're more inclined to trust the brand that created this content. It's not just another article; it's a conversation that speaks directly to your needs and concerns.

This is the essence of effective content marketing. It's not merely about churning out articles, videos, or social media posts in hopes of catching someone's attention. Instead, it's about crafting content that deeply resonates with your audience, aligning with their journey, their interests, and their emotions. When done right, content marketing becomes a powerful tool for storytelling—one that offers genuine value at every stage of your audience's experience, from initial awareness to loyal advocacy.

To harness the full potential of content marketing, begin by focusing on a specific segment of your audience. This could be a particular demographic, a niche group with specific interests, or a customer segment facing unique challenges. Understand their needs, pain points, and what motivates them. This understanding is the foundation upon which you'll build content that doesn't just inform but connects on a personal level.

With this knowledge in hand, create a piece of content tailored specifically to this segment. Whether it's a blog post that delves into solutions for their specific problems, a video that showcases how your product can improve their lives, or a social media series that inspires and engages them, the key is to tell a story that resonates. This story should reflect their journey, acknowledging their struggles, celebrating their successes, and offering value that helps them along the way.

For example, if your audience segment consists of young professionals looking to advance their careers, your content could take the form of a blog series offering actionable career advice, interviews with industry leaders, or success stories of individuals who have used your products or services to achieve their goals. Each piece of content should be crafted with the intent of guiding them, inspiring them, and ultimately, aligning your brand with their aspirations.

Once your content is live, monitor the response closely. Track engagement metrics such as clicks, shares, comments, and time spent on the page. But don't stop there—look at the qualitative feedback as well. Are people commenting that the content felt relevant or helpful? Are they sharing it within their networks? Use this data to refine your content strategy, continuously tweaking your approach to ensure that your content not only reaches but truly resonates with your audience.

By creating content that speaks directly to the needs and interests of your audience, you're doing more than just marketing—you're building trust, fostering relationships, and positioning your brand as a valuable partner in their journey. This approach doesn't just drive engagement; it creates a loyal, emotionally connected audience that sees your brand as an essential part of their lives.

Chapter 7: The Power of Testimonials and Case Studies

Before making a significant purchase, do you find yourself scouring reviews online or turning to friends for their opinions? It's a natural instinct to seek out the experiences of others who have faced similar decisions. The words and stories of those who have already walked the path you're considering can have a profound impact on your own choices. Whether it's the enthusiastic recommendation of a friend or the detailed account of a satisfied customer, these shared experiences often provide the reassurance and confidence needed to move forward.

Testimonials and case studies are powerful forms of storytelling that leverage this influence to build trust and credibility. They are more than just endorsements; they are narratives that showcase real-world results and genuine satisfaction. When potential customers read or hear about the positive experiences of others—people who once stood in their shoes and chose your brand—they're more likely to trust in the value and reliability of what you offer. These stories bridge the gap between skepticism and belief, turning potential interest into actionable confidence.

To harness the power of testimonials and case studies, start by identifying one or two customers who have had particularly positive experiences with your brand. These should be individuals who are not only satisfied with your product or service but who also represent your ideal customer profile. Reach out to them and ask if they'd be willing to share their story—how they discovered your brand, the challenges they faced, how your product or service helped them overcome those challenges, and the results they achieved.

With their permission, craft a compelling case study or testimonial that highlights their journey. This isn't just about listing benefits or features; it's about telling a story that others can see themselves in. Begin with the customer's initial situation or problem—something relatable that others in your target audience might also be experiencing. Then, detail how your brand stepped in as the solution, providing specific examples of how your product or service made a difference. Finally, showcase the positive outcomes—the tangible results, the improved quality of life, the success they've achieved as a result of using your brand.

Once you've created this testimonial or case study, share it widely. Feature it prominently on your website's homepage or in a dedicated testimonials section. Post it on your social media channels, perhaps as a series of posts that break down the customer's journey step by step. Consider incorporating it into your email marketing campaigns or even as part of a presentation in sales meetings. The goal is to ensure that this story reaches as many potential customers as possible, showing them real proof of your brand's value.

Finally, track the impact of these testimonials and case studies on your business. Monitor metrics like website traffic, time spent on your testimonials page, social media engagement, and, most importantly, conversion rates. Are people spending more time exploring your offerings after reading these stories? Are they more likely to make a purchase? Use this data to refine your approach, potentially creating more case studies and testimonials that speak to different segments of your audience.

By showcasing the real-world successes of your customers, you're not just telling people that your brand is trustworthy—you're showing them. This approach transforms abstract promises into concrete proof, making your brand more relatable, credible, and ultimately, more persuasive. In a marketplace filled with choices, it's these authentic stories that will set your brand apart and guide potential customers toward choosing you with confidence.

Chapter 8: The Art of Persuasive Copywriting

Words have the power to move mountains—or at the very least, move people to take action. Think about it: a headline that immediately grabs your attention, a compelling offer that piques your interest, or a call to action so irresistible that you feel almost compelled to click. These aren't just random strokes of luck; they are the results of strategic, persuasive copywriting, a powerful tool in your marketing arsenal that can transform casual browsers into engaged customers.

Persuasive copywriting goes far beyond just good grammar or a clever turn of phrase. It's an art form rooted in psychology, an understanding of what makes your audience tick. It's about tapping into their desires, addressing their fears, and speaking directly to their motivations. Effective copy doesn't just inform—it resonates on an emotional level, creating a connection that drives action.

To truly harness the power of persuasive copywriting, start by analyzing a piece of marketing copy you've written recently. Whether it's an email, a social media post, a landing page, or an advertisement, take a critical look at the language you've used. Ask yourself: Does this copy speak directly to my audience's needs and wants? Does it create a sense of urgency that makes the reader feel they must act now rather than later? Does it clearly highlight the benefits of what you're offering, rather than just listing features? And most importantly, does it end with a strong, clear call to action that leaves no doubt about what the next step should be?

Once you've assessed your original copy, it's time to rewrite it with a laser focus on persuasion. Start by creating urgency. This doesn't mean using gimmicks or false scarcity, but rather, emphasizing why the reader should care—and care right now. Perhaps it's a limited-time offer, a special promotion, or the fact that your product or service can solve a pressing problem they're currently facing. Use words and phrases that convey immediacy, like "don't miss out," "only available today," or "limited spots remaining."

Next, shift your focus to benefits rather than features. Your audience isn't just interested in what your product or service is; they want to know what it can do for them. How will it improve their life, save them time, or make their job easier? Speak to these benefits directly and clearly. For example, instead of saying "Our software has a user-friendly interface," you might say "Spend less time learning and more time achieving your goals with our intuitive software."

Finally, end with a powerful call to action. This is where you tell your audience exactly what to do next. But don't just tell them—compel them. Use action-oriented language that conveys confidence and direction. Instead of a generic "Click here," try something more specific and enticing, like "Get started today" or "Claim your exclusive offer now."

After you've rewritten your copy, put it to the test. Compare the revised version against the original in a real-world scenario. This could be through an A/B test in an email campaign, a split test on a landing page, or comparing engagement rates on social media posts. Pay close attention to the results: which version generates more clicks, conversions, or overall engagement?

By refining your approach and focusing on persuasive techniques, you're not just improving your copy—you're enhancing your ability to connect with your audience on a deeper level. Effective copywriting is about more than just words on a page; it's about crafting messages that move people, inspire action, and ultimately, drive the success of your brand.

Chapter 9: Building Community Through Stories

Imagine being part of a community where everyone shares a passion that resonates deeply within you. It's a place where stories are exchanged, experiences are celebrated, and every interaction reinforces a collective identity. In this space, you feel a profound sense of belonging, knowing that others understand your journey and that you're part of something bigger. This connection doesn't just make you loyal to the community—it also strengthens your loyalty to the brand that brought you all together.

Building a community around your brand is one of the most powerful ways to transform customers into advocates and create a dedicated, loyal following. It's not just about selling a product or service; it's about creating a space where your audience feels understood, valued, and connected. By sharing stories that resonate with their values, interests, and experiences, you can cultivate a sense of belonging that makes your brand more than just a name—it becomes a shared experience, a trusted companion on their journey.

To begin, identify a platform or space where your audience naturally gathers. This could be a social media group where discussions flow freely, a forum dedicated to your industry or niche, or even an email list where your most engaged customers receive regular updates. The key is to find a space where your audience feels comfortable and open to interaction—a place they consider a go-to resource for the topics that matter most to them.

Once you've identified this space, start by sharing your brand's story. This isn't just a corporate history lesson—it's a narrative that highlights your brand's values, mission, and the journey that led you to where you are today. Be authentic and transparent, showing the human side of your brand. What challenges have you overcome? What drives your passion? How does your brand align with the values and aspirations of your community? This story sets the stage for deeper connections, inviting your audience to see themselves in your brand's journey.

But don't stop there. Encourage members of your community to share their own stories as well. Whether it's how they discovered your brand, how they use your products or services in their daily lives, or how your brand has made a difference for them, these personal stories add richness and diversity to the community narrative. They transform the brand-customer relationship from a one-way street into a dynamic, interactive conversation.

Engage with your community regularly, not just as a brand, but as a member of the community. Respond to comments, join discussions, and show genuine interest in the stories being shared. Share content that is relevant and valuable, and that reinforces the themes that resonate most with your audience. The more you participate, the stronger the connections will become.

As you nurture this community, observe how storytelling strengthens the bond between your brand and your audience. You'll likely notice an increase in engagement, as members feel more connected to the brand and to each other. Watch for signs of advocacy—when members start recommending your brand to others, defending it, or sharing their positive experiences unprompted. This is the true power of community: it turns customers into champions for your brand, creating a loyal following that is deeply invested in your success.

By building and nurturing a community around your brand, you're not just fostering customer loyalty—you're creating a network of advocates who share your brand's story far and wide. This community becomes a living, breathing extension of your brand, one that grows and evolves with the people who are part of it. In this space, your brand is more than just a product or service; it's a shared journey, a common bond, and a source of belonging.

Chapter 10: Storytelling on Social Media

Have you ever found yourself in the middle of an endless scroll through your social media feed, only to be stopped in your tracks by a single post that grabs your attention? Maybe it was a striking image, a captivating caption, or a story that resonated with you so deeply that you couldn't help but pause and take it all in. These moments of connection are what make social media such a powerful tool for storytelling—it's where stories don't just exist but come to life, unfolding in real-time as they engage, inspire, and provoke thought.

Social media platforms offer unparalleled opportunities for brands to tell their stories in ways that are dynamic, interactive, and perfectly tailored to their audience. Each platform comes with its own unique features and strengths, allowing you to craft stories that are not only platform-specific but also highly engaging and shareable. Instagram, with its visual-centric approach, invites you to tell stories through compelling images and videos, enhanced by captions that add depth and context. Twitter, with its character limits, challenges you to be concise, to the point, and impactful, turning brevity into a form of art. Meanwhile, platforms like Facebook and LinkedIn offer spaces for longer narratives, where you can dive deeper into your brand's story, sharing updates, articles, and user-generated content that foster community and discussion.

This chapter delves into the art of crafting stories that resonate on social media, focusing on how to tailor your approach to the unique strengths of each platform. It's not just about posting content—it's about creating a narrative that unfolds over time, each post adding a new layer to the story you're telling. By doing so, you can build a strong and cohesive social media presence that not only engages your audience but also encourages them to become part of the story themselves.

To begin, choose the social media platform that is most relevant to your audience and aligns with your brand's strengths. This could be Instagram if your brand is visually driven, Twitter if you're looking to spark conversations, or LinkedIn if you're targeting professionals with in-depth content. Once you've selected your platform, create a series of posts that tell a cohesive story over the course of a week. This could be a behind-the-scenes look at your brand, a customer success story, a product launch, or even a thematic series that builds anticipation and engagement with each post.

As you roll out your series, pay close attention to how your audience responds. Track key metrics such as likes, comments, shares, and overall engagement. Are your posts sparking conversations? Are your followers sharing your content with their networks? Are you seeing an increase in followers or a deeper level of interaction? These insights are crucial for understanding the effectiveness of your storytelling approach and can help you refine your strategy for future campaigns.

But don't just focus on the numbers—listen to the stories your audience is telling in response to your content. Are they sharing their own experiences? Are they engaging with your brand's narrative in meaningful ways? This two-way storytelling is what makes social media so powerful.

Chapter 11: Authenticity in Storytelling

Have you ever felt disappointed by a brand that failed to live up to the promises it made? It's a frustrating experience, one that can leave you questioning your loyalty and trust in that brand. When a brand's story—the narrative it shares with the world—doesn't align with its actions, the disconnect becomes glaringly obvious. Trust is broken, and more often than not, customers walk away, taking their loyalty and business elsewhere.

In the realm of storytelling, authenticity is everything. It's the foundation upon which effective storytelling is built, and without it, even the most polished narrative can crumble under scrutiny. We live in an era where consumers are more discerning and skeptical than ever before. They have access to endless information, and they are quick to spot when a brand's words don't match its deeds. In this landscape, being genuine and transparent isn't just a nice-to-have; it's a necessity.

To ensure that your brand's story is not just compelling but also credible, start by taking a critical look at your existing narrative and marketing materials. Ask yourself: Are these materials truly representative of who we are as a brand? Do they accurately reflect our values, mission, and the promises we make to our customers? It's important to be honest in this assessment—acknowledging areas where your story may have drifted from reality is the first step toward realignment.

If you find discrepancies, make the necessary adjustments to bring your story back into alignment with your brand's actions. This might mean refining your messaging to better reflect your core values, or it could involve making changes to your operations, customer service, or product offerings to ensure they live up to the story you're telling. Authenticity isn't about perfection; it's about consistency and integrity—making sure that what you say matches what you do.

Once you've revised your story to ensure it's authentic and aligned with your brand's actions, share it with your audience. Be transparent about the changes you've made and why they were necessary. This openness not only reinforces your commitment to honesty but also helps rebuild trust with your audience. People appreciate when brands are willing to admit their shortcomings and take steps to improve. It shows that you're listening, learning, and evolving.

After sharing your revised story, observe how it impacts your audience's perception of your brand. Monitor engagement levels, feedback, and overall sentiment. Are customers responding positively to your authenticity? Are they more engaged with your brand's content and more likely to share it within their networks?

These indicators will give you valuable insights into how well your authentic storytelling is resonating.

Remember, authenticity is an ongoing commitment, not a one-time fix. Continuously ensure that your brand's actions align with its story, and be prepared to make adjustments as needed. By consistently living up to your promises, you'll build a strong foundation of trust, one that fosters long-term loyalty and sets your brand apart in a crowded marketplace. In the end, it's not just about telling a good story—it's about being the brand that customers can believe in.

Chapter 12: The Role of Customer Feedback in Your Story

Imagine having a direct line to your customers, where they openly share their thoughts, experiences, and perceptions of your brand. Picture the invaluable insights you'd gain from this unfiltered feedback—insights that could not only confirm what you're doing right but also highlight areas where you could improve. Now, imagine harnessing this feedback to refine and shape your brand story, making it even more compelling, authentic, and in tune with the very people you're trying to reach.

Customer feedback is more than just a tool for gauging satisfaction; it's a goldmine of insights that can help you evolve your brand story to better align with your audience's values, needs, and expectations. In a world where consumers have more power and voice than ever before, listening to them isn't just beneficial—it's essential. By tapping into this resource, you can ensure your brand narrative remains relevant, resonates deeply, and builds stronger connections with your customers.

To start, consider creating a simple yet effective survey or feedback form designed to gather your customers' opinions about your brand story and overall marketing efforts. This doesn't need to be an extensive questionnaire—sometimes, a few well-crafted questions can provide more valuable insights than a lengthy survey.

Focus on asking questions that reveal how your customers perceive your brand's narrative, what they find most engaging, and where they see room for improvement. For example:

- *How would you describe our brand in three words?*
- *What aspects of our brand story resonate most with you?*
- *Is there anything about our marketing that you find unclear or unappealing?*
- *How could we better align our brand story with your values or needs?*

Distribute this survey across various touchpoints—whether it's through email, social media, or directly on your website—to ensure you reach a broad segment of your audience. Encourage honest feedback by making it clear that their opinions are valued and will directly influence the future of your brand.

Once you've gathered the responses, take the time to analyze them thoroughly. Look for common themes or recurring suggestions that stand out across different customer segments. Are there particular aspects of your brand story that customers consistently praise? Are there elements that they find confusing or disconnected from their expectations? This analysis will give you a clearer picture of how your brand is currently perceived and where adjustments might be needed.

With these insights in hand, use the feedback to make strategic adjustments to your brand narrative. This might involve refining your messaging to better reflect the values that resonate most with your audience or simplifying complex aspects of your story that customers find difficult to understand. Perhaps you'll discover that your audience values a particular aspect of your brand that you hadn't emphasized enough—this could be an opportunity to bring that element to the forefront of your narrative.

As you refine your brand story based on this feedback, remember to communicate these changes to your audience. Let them know that their voices were heard and that you've made specific adjustments to better meet their expectations. This not only shows that you value their input but also helps reinforce the connection between your brand and its audience, making them feel like active participants in your brand's journey.

Finally, monitor the impact of these changes. Keep an eye on key metrics such as engagement, customer loyalty, and overall brand sentiment to see how well your revised story resonates with your audience. Continuously gather feedback and be open to further adjustments—your brand story should evolve alongside your customers, reflecting their changing needs and the dynamic world around them.

By actively involving your customers in the shaping of your brand story, you're not just telling a story—you're creating a collaborative narrative that reflects the voices, values, and aspirations of the people who matter most to your brand. This approach doesn't just make your story more compelling; it makes it more authentic, more relevant, and ultimately, more powerful.

Chapter 13: Storytelling in Email Marketing

Picture this: you open your inbox and there, among the usual clutter of promotions and notifications, is an email that immediately catches your eye. The subject line piques your curiosity, and as you open it, you're drawn into a narrative that feels personal—almost as if it was crafted just for you. The story it tells is so captivating, so relevant to your interests or needs, that you can't help but read on. Before you know it, you're eagerly clicking through to explore more, feeling a genuine connection to the message and the brand behind it.

This is the power of storytelling in email marketing. Unlike other forms of digital communication, email offers a direct, intimate channel to your audience's attention, making it the perfect platform for weaving compelling narratives that resonate on a personal level. When done right, an email isn't just a message in a bottle—it's a story that builds relationships, drives engagement, and ultimately, leads to conversions.

To harness this potential, start by reflecting on your most recent email campaign. Ask yourself: Did it tell a story? Did it go beyond simply delivering information or promoting a product? If the answer is no, you may have missed an opportunity to truly connect with your audience. A great email does more than just sell—it invites the reader into a narrative where they are the hero, guided by your brand through a journey of discovery, problem-solving, or inspiration.

Now, it's time to craft a new email with storytelling at its heart. Begin by identifying the core message or goal of your email—what do you want your readers to feel, know, or do by the end of it? Then, think about how you can frame this message within a story. Perhaps you can share a customer success story, illustrating how your product or service helped someone achieve their goals. Or maybe you can draw the reader in with a behind-the-scenes look at your brand, showing the passion and craftsmanship that goes into what you do.

As you write, focus on creating a narrative arc that guides the reader through the email. Start with a compelling opening that grabs attention—this could be a relatable scenario, a surprising fact, or a provocative question. Next, build the story by addressing the reader's needs or interests, using language that speaks directly to them. Engage their emotions by highlighting challenges they may face and showing how your brand can provide the solution. Finally, conclude with a clear and persuasive call to action, leading them to take the next step, whether it's clicking through to your website, making a purchase, or signing up for more information.

Once your storytelling email is ready, send it out and monitor its performance closely. Track key metrics like open rates, click-through rates, and overall engagement. Compare these metrics with those from your previous, non-storytelling emails. Are more people opening and reading your email? Are they engaging with the content and taking the desired action?

Pay attention to any feedback you receive, whether it's direct responses from recipients or comments on social media. This qualitative data can provide deeper insights into how your story resonated with your audience and how you might further refine your approach.

Remember, the goal of storytelling in email marketing isn't just to increase metrics—it's to build a stronger, more meaningful connection with your audience. By consistently incorporating stories into your email campaigns, you're not just communicating with your customers; you're inviting them to be part of your brand's journey, creating a sense of loyalty and engagement that goes far beyond a single transaction.

In the end, an email that tells a story is more than just another piece of marketing—it's a narrative that draws your audience in, makes them feel valued, and motivates them to act. It's about making each reader feel like they're not just a name on a list, but an important part of a story that's still unfolding.

Chapter 14: Storytelling for Small Budgets

You don't need deep pockets to tell a compelling story. In fact, some of the most memorable and successful marketing campaigns have been built not on the foundation of large budgets, but on creativity, resourcefulness, and a deep understanding of the audience. These campaigns prove that it's not the size of your budget that matters, but the power of your ideas and the authenticity of your message.

For small businesses and entrepreneurs who often operate with limited marketing resources, this is an encouraging reality. While you may not have the funds to launch a high-profile ad campaign or produce glossy commercials, you have something equally valuable: the ability to craft stories that resonate deeply with your audience, stories that can be shared, appreciated, and acted upon without the need for significant financial investment.

The key to success lies in identifying and leveraging low-cost storytelling tactics that can deliver high-impact results. These tactics rely more on creativity and strategic thinking than on money, allowing you to connect with your audience in meaningful ways while staying within your budget.

Start by exploring a low-cost storytelling tactic that you haven't tried yet. For instance, creating behind-the-scenes videos is a powerful way to humanize your brand and give your audience a glimpse into the inner workings of your business. These videos don't need to be professionally produced to be effective; often, a simple, authentic video shot on a smartphone can be just as engaging, if not more so, than a polished production. Show your audience the people behind the brand, the process of creating your products, or the day-to-day life at your company. This transparency fosters trust and builds a personal connection with your audience.

Another cost-effective tactic is to encourage user-generated content (UGC). This approach not only saves you the cost of content creation but also leverages the power of your community. By inviting your customers to share their experiences with your brand—whether through photos, videos, or stories—you create a wealth of authentic content that resonates with potential customers. UGC serves as social proof, showing that real people enjoy and endorse your products or services, which can significantly boost your brand's credibility and appeal.

Partnering with influencers is another strategy that can be highly effective, even on a limited budget. While big-name influencers may be out of reach, there are countless micro-influencers who have smaller, but highly engaged, followings. These influencers often have more authentic relationships with their audiences and can deliver your brand's story in a way that feels personal and genuine.

By partnering with micro-influencers, you can tap into their trusted networks and reach new audiences without the hefty price tag.

Once you've selected a tactic, implement it into your marketing strategy and track its impact on engagement and brand awareness. Use analytics tools to monitor key metrics such as social media engagement, website traffic, and conversion rates. Are your behind-the-scenes videos driving more views and shares? Is user-generated content increasing your social media engagement and bringing in new followers? Are your influencer partnerships translating into higher brand visibility and sales?

Don't just look at the numbers—listen to the qualitative feedback as well. What are your customers saying in the comments? Are they more engaged with your brand's story? Do they feel a stronger connection to your business? These insights are crucial in understanding the effectiveness of your storytelling efforts and can guide you in refining your approach.

Remember, powerful storytelling isn't about the amount of money you spend—it's about the authenticity, creativity, and relevance of the stories you tell. By focusing on low-cost, high-impact tactics, you can create campaigns that resonate deeply with your audience, build brand loyalty, and drive real results, all without breaking the bank. In the end, it's not about the size of your budget, but the strength of your story that truly makes an impact.

Chapter 15: Measuring the Impact of Your Story

How do you know if your story is truly resonating with your audience? In a world overflowing with content, it's not enough to simply tell a story—you need to ensure that it's connecting with your audience on a deeper level. But how can you gauge the effectiveness of your storytelling? What specific metrics can you rely on to determine whether your narrative is striking the right chords, driving engagement, and ultimately, achieving your goals?

Measuring the impact of your storytelling isn't just a nice-to-have; it's essential. Without clear metrics to evaluate success, you're essentially flying blind, unsure of what's working and what isn't. By diligently analyzing key performance indicators, you can uncover valuable insights into which elements of your storytelling resonate most with your audience and identify areas where your approach may need adjustment.

To begin, choose a storytelling campaign you've recently launched. This could be anything from a social media series to an email marketing initiative, a video campaign, or even a content-driven website update. Once you've selected the campaign, it's time to identify the key metrics that will help you measure its success. The metrics you choose should align with your campaign's objectives and the platforms you're using.

Here are some key metrics to consider:

1. **Engagement Metrics**: These include likes, shares, comments, retweets, and overall interaction with your content. Engagement metrics are a direct indicator of how your audience is reacting to your story. High engagement suggests that your story is resonating, sparking conversation, and encouraging users to share it within their own networks. Low engagement, on the other hand, may indicate that your story isn't connecting as intended.

2. **View and Read Metrics**: For video content, track metrics like total views, view duration, and completion rates. For written content, consider metrics like time spent on the page, scroll depth, and bounce rate. These metrics reveal how compelling your story is—are people sticking around to watch the entire video or read through the entire article? If they're leaving early, it could be a sign that your story isn't holding their attention.

3. **Click-Through Rates (CTR)**: If your story includes a call to action, such as a link to learn more, sign up, or make a purchase, tracking the click-through rate is crucial. A high CTR indicates that your story is not only engaging but also motivating your audience to take the desired action.

4. **Conversion Metrics**: Ultimately, the goal of many storytelling campaigns is to drive conversions, whether that's making a purchase, signing up for a newsletter, or filling out a contact form. Conversion metrics show how effectively your story is moving your audience down the funnel. Are they inspired to take the next step after engaging with your content?

5. **Sentiment Analysis**: Beyond numbers, understanding the sentiment behind comments, reviews, and social media mentions is vital. Tools that analyze sentiment can help you gauge the emotional impact of your story. Are people reacting positively, expressing excitement, or sharing their personal connections to your story? Or are they indifferent, confused, or even negative?

6. **Customer Feedback**: Direct feedback from your audience can be incredibly valuable. Consider conducting surveys or simply encouraging comments that ask how your content resonated with them. This qualitative data can provide context to the quantitative metrics and offer insights that numbers alone can't.

Once you've identified the key metrics for your campaign, track them diligently over the course of a month. Pay close attention to trends—are certain days or times driving more engagement? Are specific pieces of content within the campaign performing better than others? Look for patterns that can inform your understanding of what's resonating with your audience.

After collecting and analyzing the data, use these insights to refine your future storytelling efforts. Focus on the elements that performed well—perhaps it was the emotional tone of your story, the authenticity of the characters, or the clarity of the narrative. Conversely, identify areas for improvement and adjust your strategy accordingly.

By consistently measuring and analyzing the impact of your storytelling, you can craft narratives that not only captivate your audience but also drive meaningful results for your brand. In the end, the success of your story isn't just in the telling—it's in how deeply it resonates, how widely it's shared, and how effectively it inspires action.

Conclusion: Your Storytelling Journey Begins

Congratulations on completing this guide to storytelling in marketing! This is a significant milestone, but remember, the art of storytelling is not a one-time endeavor—it's a continuous, evolving journey. As you move forward, keep in mind that your brand's narrative is a living, breathing entity. It needs to grow and adapt alongside your business, your audience, and the ever-changing landscape of the market.

Storytelling is about more than just crafting a single compelling narrative; it's about consistently communicating your brand's values, understanding your audience's needs and emotions, and being flexible enough to evolve your story as your brand and your customers evolve. The stories you tell have the potential to leave a lasting impact, shaping how your brand is perceived and remembered. Now, armed with the insights and strategies from this guide, it's time to take your story and share it with the world.

Follow-Up Activities:

1. **Host a Workshop with Your Team:** Gather your team for a dedicated workshop to refine and deepen your brand's story using the strategies and techniques you've learned. Start by revisiting your brand's history, mission, and values. Identify the key moments that

have defined your journey, the challenges you've overcome, and the victories you've celebrated. Use these elements to build a rich, multi-dimensional narrative that authentically represents who you are and what you stand for. Encourage collaboration and creativity—each team member can offer unique perspectives that enrich the story. By the end of the workshop, you should have a clearly defined brand narrative that resonates with both your internal team and your external audience.

2. **Plan a Month's Worth of Content:** Take your newly refined brand story and translate it into a comprehensive content plan for the next month. Your goal is to ensure consistency and coherence across all platforms. This plan should include a diverse mix of content types—blog posts that dive into your brand's mission and values, social media updates that tell mini-stories or highlight customer experiences, emails that engage and inform, and visuals that capture the essence of your brand in a glance. Each piece of content should align with your brand story, reinforcing the key messages you want to communicate. Use this content plan not only to tell your story but to create a narrative arc that keeps your audience engaged over time.

3. **Set Up a System for Regular Customer Feedback:** Implement a system to consistently gather and analyze feedback from your customers. This feedback is invaluable—it provides real-time insights into how your brand story is being received and perceived. Whether it's through surveys, social media interactions, or direct conversations, make it a priority to listen to your audience. Use their feedback to refine your story, ensuring it remains relevant, resonant, and responsive to their needs. By staying attuned to your customers' voices, you can keep your narrative dynamic and adaptable, continually strengthening the connection between your brand and its audience.

Your journey as a storyteller in marketing is just beginning. With the tools, strategies, and insights outlined in this guide, you are well-equipped to craft stories that are not only powerful but also memorable—stories that connect with your audience on a deep level and drive your brand forward with authenticity and purpose.

As you continue to develop your storytelling skills, remember that the most successful stories are those that stay true to your brand's core values while also embracing change and innovation. Keep experimenting, keep learning, and most importantly, keep telling your story. The world is ready to listen, and your narrative has the power to inspire, engage, and create lasting impact.